MW00986124

By:

OOLS
HON

Yellow Umbrella Books are published by Capstone Press
151 Good Counsel Drive, P.O. Box 669, Mankato, Minnesota 56002
http://www.capstone-press.com

Library of Congress Cataloging-in-Publication Data
Trumbauer, Lisa, 1963-
    Everyone is a scientist/by Lisa Trumbauer; consultant editor, Gail Saunders-Smith.
    p. cm.
    Includes index.
    ISBN 0-7368-0722-5
    1. Science—Juvenile literature. 2. Scientists—Juvenile literature. [1. Scientists.
2. Occupations.] I. Saunders-Smith, Gail. II. Title.
Q126.4.T74   2001
500—dc21   00-036804

    Summary: Describes what a scientist does and the tools a scientist uses. Explains that
    different types of scientists do different jobs.

Editorial Credits:
Susan Evento, Managing Editor/Product Development; Elizabeth Jaffe, Senior Editor;
    Jannike Hess, Designer; Kimberly Danger and Heidi Schoof, Photo Researchers

Photo Credits:
Cover: David F. Clobes; Title Page: Jackson Smith/Pictor; Page 2: Visuals Unlimited/Jeff Daly;
Page 3: Photo Network/Eric Berndt; Page 4: Llewellyn/Pictor; Page 5: Unicorn Stock
Photos/Karen Holsinger Mullen; Page 6: Nelson/Pictor; Page 7: Visuals Unlimited/Bill Beatty;
Page 8: Visuals Unlimited/W.J. Weber; Page 9: Photri-Microstock/Dennis MacDonald; Page 10:
David Austen/Pictor; Page 11: International Stock/Elliott Smith; Page 12: Visuals
Unlimited/Rob Simpson; Page 13: Bob Daemmrich/Pictor; Page 14: Visuals Unlimited/Jeff
Greenberg (top), Kent & Donna Dannen (bottom); Page 15: Richard Hamilton Smith (top), Bob
Daemmrich/Pictor (bottom); Page 16: Unicorn Stock Photos/Karen Holsinger Mullen

1 2 3 4 5 6 06 05 04 03 02 01

Everyone Is a Scientist

Trumbauer,
Lisa

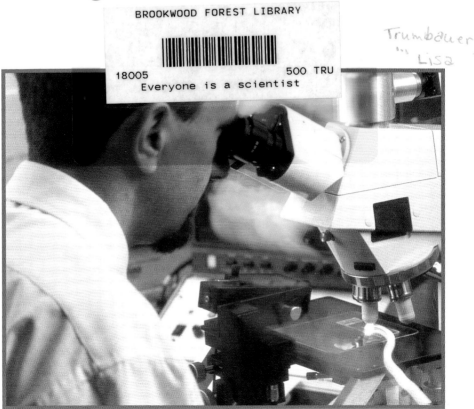

Consulting Editor: Gail Saunders-Smith, Ph.D.
Consultants: Claudine Jellison and Patricia Williams,
Reading Recovery Teachers
Content Consultant: Vivian O'Dell,
Staff Scientist at Fermi National Accelerator Lab

Yellow Umbrella Books

an imprint of Capstone Press
Mankato, Minnesota

A scientist is someone
who learns about how
the world works.
This scientist looks closely
at plants to learn
more about them.

These scientists look
closely at a caterpillar
to learn more about it.

Scientists learn about the world by asking questions. This scientist asks questions about why this liquid turns red.

These scientists ask questions about the different sea animals they will find in this water.

Scientists learn about the
world by using tools.
This scientist uses
a microscope to see
very small things up close.

This scientist uses
a magnifying glass to see
these flowers up close.

Scientists use tools that measure.
This scientist uses tools
that measure the growth
of an egg.

This scientist uses tools to measure liquids for his experiment.

Scientists often work together
in teams.
These scientists work together
to find rocks that are
deep in the ground.

These scientists work together
to learn more about this apple.

Scientists write down facts and

share what they have learned.

Some scientists learn about plants and animals.

Some scientists learn about Earth—its land, water, and sky.

And some scientists learn about how things work.

When are you a scientist?

Words to Know/Index

Earth—the planet on which we live; page 15

experiment—a test used to prove something in science; page 9

liquid—something wet that flows freely; pages 4, 9

magnifying glass—a lens that makes things look bigger; a person usually holds a magnifying glass in the hand; page 7

measure—to find out the exact size or weight of something; pages 8, 9

microscope—a tool with several lenses that makes very small things look bigger; page 6

scientist—a person who studies and questions the nature of things in the world; pages 2, 3, 4, 5, 6, 7, 8, 9, 10, 11, 12, 14, 15, 16

tool—an item that is used to do work; tools are usually held in the hand; pages 6, 8, 9

Word Count: 194
Early Intervention Levels: 9–12